ANIMAL EXTREMES

STRANGEST SENSES

BY ASHLEY GISH

WWW.APEXEDITIONS.COM

Apex is distributed by North Star Editions:
sales@northstareditions.com | 888-417-0195

Produced for Apex by Red Line Editorial.

Photographs ©: Shutterstock Images, cover, 1, 6–7, 8, 9, 10–11, 12–13, 14, 15, 16–17, 18, 19, 20–21, 22–23, 26–27, 29, iStockphoto, 4–5; Ali Bayless/NMFS/PIFSC/NOAA, 24; LCDR Eric Johnson/NOAA Corps/NOAA, 25

Library of Congress Control Number: 2022919896

ISBN
978-1-63738-533-3 (hardcover)
978-1-63738-587-6 (paperback)
978-1-63738-694-1 (ebook pdf)
978-1-63738-641-5 (hosted ebook)

Printed in the United States of America
Mankato, MN
082023

NOTE TO PARENTS AND EDUCATORS

Apex books are designed to build literacy skills in striving readers. Exciting, high-interest content attracts and holds readers' attention. The text is carefully leveled to allow students to achieve success quickly. Additional features, such as bolded glossary words for difficult terms, help build comprehension.

TABLE OF CONTENTS

CHAPTER 1

CAVE BIRDS

The sun goes down. Oilbirds have been resting inside a cave. Now they fly out to search for food.

Oilbirds are active mainly at night. They fly many miles looking for fruit to eat.

Oilbirds live in caves in South America.

Both the cave and the night are pitch-dark. But oilbirds have no trouble getting around. They use whiskers on their faces to feel the cave's walls.

STAYING HIDDEN

In the past, people hunted oilbirds. They used the birds' fat for food or **fuel**. Thousands of oilbirds were killed. But the birds that lived deepest inside caves survived.

Oilbirds also use **echolocation** as they fly. They send out a series of clicks. The sounds bounce back and help the birds sense their surroundings.

Other than oilbirds, swiftlets are the only birds known to use echolocation.

FAST FACT

Several animals use echolocation. They include bats, dolphins, and a few other **mammals**.

Oilbirds use echolocation to learn the shapes and sizes of things around them.

CHAPTER 2

Butterflies taste with their feet. This helps them find safe plants to lay eggs on. Other insects have ears on their bellies or legs.

Katydids have ears on their knees.

Whip spiders use their sense of smell to find food or get back home.

Whip spiders have very long front legs. The tips of these legs act like **antennae**. They pick up scents from the air and ground. Whip spiders use the smells to know where to go.

A snake's tongue can pick up smells from the air or ground.

A snake gathers scents by flicking its tongue. The tongue touches an organ inside the snake's mouth. This organ identifies the different smells.

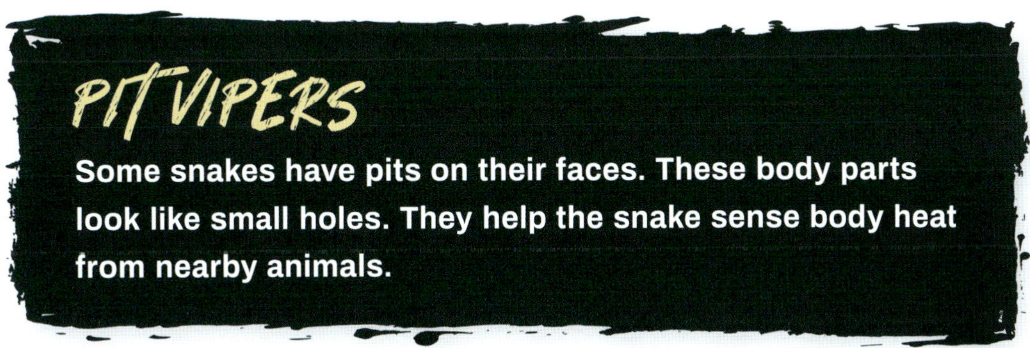

PIT VIPERS

Some snakes have pits on their faces. These body parts look like small holes. They help the snake sense body heat from nearby animals.

A pit viper's heat-sensing pits are between its eyes and nostrils.

CHAPTER 3

UNUSUAL EYESIGHT

Bees can see ultraviolet light. This type of light is invisible to humans. But bees use it to find **nectar** in flowers.

Many flowers have ultraviolet patterns on their petals. These patterns show bees where nectar is.

Mantis shrimp see many types of light. This helps them see **prey** that move fast. The shrimp jump quickly to grab the prey.

Mantis shrimp punch their prey with their front legs to kill the prey.

A blind cave fish's lateral line helps the fish find food and not run into things.

NO NEED FOR EYES

Blind cave fish do not have eyes. Instead, they have a lateral line. This line runs along the side of the fish's body. It senses movement in the water.

Two large front eyes help jumping spiders see color. Two smaller front eyes see in black and white.

Jumping spiders have eight eyes. Four eyes face forward. And four are on the sides of their heads. These side eyes help the spiders see almost all the way behind their bodies.

CHAPTER 4

UNIQUE ABILITIES

A platypus uses its bill to find prey in murky water. The bill senses electricity that is sent out by animals' bodies.

Platypuses mainly eat tiny water creatures. But they sometimes eat fish or frogs.

Adult sea turtles often live alone.

Sea turtles can sense Earth's **magnetic field**. It helps them find their way as they swim.

GOING HOME

A female sea turtle lays eggs on the same beach each year. Her babies will return to this beach to lay eggs of their own.

Some types of turtles only lay eggs every couple of years.

Thousands of monarchs fly south from the United States to Mexico each year.

Monarch butterflies sense Earth's magnetic field, too. It helps them find their way when flying long distances. Monarchs also track where the sun is in the sky.

FAST FACT

Monarch butterflies **migrate** south each fall. Some travel up to 3,000 miles (4,800 km).

COMPREHENSION QUESTIONS

Write your answers on a separate piece of paper.

1. Write a few sentences describing one thing that helps oilbirds find their way in the dark.
2. If you could have one of the senses described in this book, which one would you want? Why?
3. What do blind cavefish use to sense movement in the water?
   - A. lateral line
   - B. echolocation
   - C. antennae
4. How would sensing body heat from nearby animals help pit vipers?
   - A. It would help the vipers hide.
   - B. It would help the vipers not get lost.
   - C. It would help the vipers find prey.

5. What does **survived** mean in this book?

Thousands of oilbirds were killed. But the birds that lived deepest inside caves ***survived****.*

A. died out
B. stayed living
C. changed shape

6. What does **identifies** mean in this book?

The tongue touches an organ inside the snake's mouth. This organ ***identifies*** *the different smells.*

A. finds what something is
B. tells what something costs
C. sees where something goes

Answer key on page 32.

GLOSSARY

antennae

Long, thin body parts used to sense surroundings.

arachnid

A type of animal with a hard outer body and eight legs, such as a scorpion or spider.

echolocation

The process of using sound to locate objects.

fuel

Something that can make power when it is burned.

magnetic field

The area around an object where its magnetic force is felt.

mammals

Animals that have hair and produce milk for their young.

migrate

To move from one part of the world to another.

nectar

A sweet liquid created by flowers.

prey

Animals that are hunted and eaten by other animals.

BOOKS

Grundmann, Emmanuelle. *When Elephants Listen with Their Feet: Discover Extraordinary Animal Senses.* Toronto: Pajama Press, 2021.

Hirsch, Rebecca E. *Sensational Senses: Amazing Ways Animals Perceive the World.* Minneapolis: Millbrook Press, 2022.

Kenney, Karen Latchana. *Platypuses.* Minneapolis: Bellwether Media, 2021.

ONLINE RESOURCES

Visit **www.apexeditions.com** to find links and resources related to this title.

ABOUT THE AUTHOR

Ashley Gish has authored more than 60 juvenile nonfiction books. She earned her degree in creative writing from Minnesota State University, Mankato. Ashley lives in Minnesota with her husband and daughter.

INDEX

ANSWER KEY:
1. Answers will vary; 2. Answers will vary; 3. A; 4. C; 5. B; 6. A